Effects of UNFAIRLY UNFAVORABLE Book Reviews on Independent Authors

When a Negative Review IS NOT MERITED by a Written Work

By: James M. Lowrance © 2012

TABLE OF HEADINGS:

1. RECENT POSITIVE AND NEGATIVE CHANGES IN PUBLISHING AND BOOK REVIEWING

2. HIGHLY NEGATIVE BOOK REVIEWS: DESTROYING AUTHORS WITH A FEW TAPS OF THE KEYBOARD

3. A BAD REVIEW ON MY HEALTH TITLE

4. ARE AUTHOR COMPLAINTS ABOUT NEGATIVE REVIEWS LEGITIMATE?

5. AUTHORS IMPROVE BUT MUST BE OPEN TO 'APPROPRIATE' CRITICISM

6. VAGUE REVIEWS NOT EXPLAINING WHY A LOW RATING WAS GIVEN

7. TRASH TITLES CONTRIBUTE TO BAD PERCEPTIONS TOWARD INDIE AUTHORS

8. IN CONCLUSION

INTRODUCTION:

Prerequisite Statement: Most book reviewers are good, honest people and just because a reviewer is harsh, this does not make them a bad or dishonest reviewer. I do believe however, that there are stark differences between harsh reviews and attack reviews or those that are directed at authors personally. I believe it is wrong for authors to attack reviewers as well. Authors should see no need in replying to reviews or reviewers, unless there is a legitimate reason to do so (very rare – usually only to point out a major mistaken perception within a book). I also do not believe authors should reply to reviewers with "thank yous", unless under special circumstances because this would mean that honest, critical reviews should also deserve a "thank you" and a bias toward positive reviews would be evident and unnecessary (readers already know that authors prefer positive reviews). Both the independent publishing and reviewing venues have good and bad things occurring within them.

As should be noted by the title of this eBook, I will mainly be addressing and discussing "unfairly unfavorable" book reviews that are posted against independent (indie) author's books and eBooks and NOT THOSE THAT ARE EARNED AND DESERVED BY THEM (negative reviews are merited in most cases, while some are 'undeserved'). Some of the content in this eBook, I have derived from posts I made on a publisher's forum, which I have rewritten and edited into headings for it. The fact that undeserved negative reviews are posted online by readers on bookseller websites, is evident by the fact that same books at the same time, can have highly favorable and positive reviews posted for them by other readers. (NOTE: This is not always a proof -- I'm pointing out a general observance, that **might indicate** that a negative review found among predominantly positive reviews, is posted for inappropriate reasons.)

This type of contrast proves that reviews are not always a matter of fact but may also a matter of taste (not posted for bogus reasons).

5

A negative perception of a written work can be held by only a small percent of readers, while a positive perception by the majority and vice versa. The point being that a negative review can sometimes stand alone or be the first type that is posted for a written work but that does not mean that it accurately reflects the quality of the book or eBook it is purported to be an accurate evaluation of.

The problem for books that are truly worthwhile and worth the price they are listed for, is that an undeserved negative review can often be the first one that appears on a book published by an indie author (NOTE: Some are not worth their price and not worthwhile -- a point I add for perspective.). This can cause a degree of reluctance for additional customers to buy an advertised product but it can also cause satisfied readers to be reluctant to add their own positive reviews. Certainly **this is not always the case** and some readers understand that their contrasted positive review can help to offset a negative one.

Unfortunately, an unsatisfied reader is more likely to post a review than is a satisfied reader and this leaves indie publishers with the need to solicit additional reviews to prevent their books and eBooks from losing more favorable ranks and positions on bookseller websites (Not all of us do this and when it does occur, the author may still be seeking honest, unbiased reviews -- others may dishonestly seek bogus favorable reviews).

Some authors resort to soliciting reviews from family, friends or fellow authors, while others will join book clubs in which they can offer their books free to customers who will review them once they complete reading them. While these methods can work well, as long as reviewers are being completely honest with their reviews, bookseller websites should also make sure that they have adequate moderation in place for review-submissions and they should screen out those that meet the definition for containing attack or spam elements within them and those that simply go overboard in the negative direction (overly-biased positive reviews are also removed by booksellers who monitor for them).

Any books or eBooks that are worthy of highly unfavorable reviews that are fairly written, should never have been approved for listing by reputable booksellers to begin with and by allowing these on their websites, they are in essence admitting to approving trash-titles for sale (NOTE: A truly bogus/trash book will be screened-out by booksellers, in the vast majority of cases). This is the reason stricter guidelines for reviews should be in place, to prevent improper perceptions from being formed by the book shopping public, toward reputable booksellers and toward the independent authors and publishers they represent. Again, I am not advocating the censorship of negative reviews that are <u>deserved</u> but against those that are obviously <u>not deserved</u> (e.g. expletive attacks toward authors and negative rants that do not reflect legitimate reviewing practices). I also hope to point out that unfavorable reviews can be stated respectfully and without an overboard abundance of negative or attack language included within them. It is a difficult subject to address but I hope to do so appropriately and in-balance, within the headings that follow.

1. RECENT POSITIVE AND NEGATIVE CHANGES IN PUBLISHING AND BOOK REVIEWING

{NOTE: I left this chapter out of this book originally. I later decided to add it as the opening chapter because I feel that changes within the industry and the way in which my own authored works became books/eBooks is important and may be of interest to this subject-matter.}

Changes in the Book Publishing Industry

It should be obvious to any objective observer, as to how dramatically the book publishing industry has changed in recent years. Rather than only the absolute best works of writing being available to interested readers (such as highest quality novels), people can now buy works of somewhat less quality but that contain information they are genuinely seeking (i.e. more of the "How To" and "Need To Know" type books and booklets). Self-publishing platforms have opened the doors for many more writers to publish their books and eBooks.

Written works containing needed knowledge or that of interest to "particular readers", can now be purchased and the fact that many of them are not in the more elite categories, is not only reflected in how they are written but also in how they are priced. Certainly an offered written work in book or eBook form, should not fall below a certain standard, otherwise it shouldn't be offered for sale by reputable bookseller stores or websites but <u>there is a place</u> for moderate-quality and narrow-niche books. There are works of acceptable quality that are not directed at wide-niche audiences, that do literally fill a need for certain readers who seek them.

Reviewers Who Order Books They Don't Like

For whom would a title like this one you are now reading be written for? My feeling is that it would be of interest to some authors who have been targeted by unethically written book reviews, posted for their works (i.e. highly negative reviews that they suspect may have been posted by competing authors). Would someone who isn't actually looking for a book of this type be disappointed in the content of it?

Yes, there is a strong possibility that it would prove to be boring content for them. Another question would be: "Do people order books for review purposes, even when they are not of particular interest to them or when they are on subjects they disagree with?" Again, yes they do, and for a variety of possible reasons. In the case of this particular book (minus this chapter), I happen to know for a fact that it was initially ordered by readers who make a practice of book-reviewing because they knew simply from the description of the book/eBook, that they disagreed with the content within it.

In their own words, they admit that they <u>would not</u> have ordered the eBook if it were not on promotional free download at the time. Can such a reviewer actually provide an unbiased review or is it even their intention to do so (I say in some cases "yes" and in some cases "no", it depends on who the reviewer is)? I will also add that comments posted under unfavorable reviews by members of the same book reviewing social community, also attacked this book but they added in their comments that they "have never read this book" or "never intend to read it".

Unfortunately, reviews by people who have never actually read a book they post negative reviews for, is also a growing problem.

Reviewers Who Don't Want to See Reviewing Oversight/Moderation

Some reviewers may feel that their practice of reviewing is being brought into question (In light of the previous subheading, why shouldn't it be?). They may also feel that in the book-reviewing arena, **anything goes** and nothing should ever be questioned in regard to reviews that are posted for books (i.e. they will cite "free speech" or "freedom of the press"). They on the other hand, may feel they have every right to question the content of the books they review. This would be a practice of no consequence for them but that might be of great consequence to the authors they may target with negative reviews. We then see that the motives and morals of reviewers, **legitimately** comes into question and it certainly should be (Should quality of content only be required on one side?).

With the advent of "reviewing websites" that are actually a form of social media, allowing members to operate under user-names, rather than under actual names like most authors do, you have what can seriously bring into question, the motives of **'some' of them**. If such a site does not uphold its own non-harassment/non-defamation TOS (Terms of Service) regarding the posting of reviews or is very lax in doing so, what defense would a targeted author have and how could such a site keep-out the bogus reviewers and bring legitimacy to their venue? This can actually be questioned for the opposite reason as well, with reviewers possibly being posted by the authors of the books they review themselves or by their friends and family members, who provide them biased positive reviews.

When oversight/moderation is missing and literal abuse is being perpetrated by a reviews venue, authors should seek the help of mediating bureaus who can investigate TOS violations if a website in question refuses to do so (i.e. The Better Business Bureau, The Administration of Bookseller Websites or the IC3).

Claiming that abuse of this type is not tolerated by a site but then allowing it to be rampant on their pages, becomes a form of false advertising. These are the thoughts and questions, with an actual basis behind them, that reveals the reasons why this is a legitimate subject to address. You would think that these things should never come into question when you consider how upset and attacking certain reviewers became when I initially released this book. They imply that it is somehow considered a taboo subject by them, that should never be addressed openly by an author (a willingness to attack from behind a user-name). My feelings on this however, come from the simple question of **how it could possibly be ignored** in light of both the new development in publishing and reviewing venues?

How I Entered Book and eBook Publishing

My story is somewhat different from that of other authors because I didn't actually set out to publish books and eBooks. My entrance into the field of writing actually occurred beginning with fellow-patient forums and message boards.

14

I developed illnesses in the year 2003 that eventually caused me to become permanently, medically disabled. Some of my conditions had definitive diagnoses placed on them with others remaining elusive to this day, as to their absolute identifications. I began to post on patient support forums when my struggles with these became severe. These venues gave those of us with similar diseases and syndromes, an opportunity to share about our symptom-struggles, our fears and our treatments. Over time, I put so much time into posting on these online meeting places, that I was eventually offered positions as a moderator on some of them. This simply meant that I would oversee the forums, to make sure they were being used for their intended purposes, being mainly that of patient support and fellowship.

After being a member of one particular forum, one fellow member suggested that I would make a great fit as editor of the connected article site whose editor was resigning.

15

The content part of the multi-topic site (information articles) was for thyroid disease patients and while it was not a paying position, it did have strict guidelines in regard to articles published. It required potential editors for it to complete training and testing, in order to obtain final approval for the position. I did complete these requirements and I was placed in the position for a period of less than two years before I resigned it, in order to write for a different online content website. During that period however, I wrote approximately 175 articles as editor over their thyroid disease topic, many of which still appear there today. This, in spite of there having been at least two other editors there since I resigned the position, whose job it was to over-write my articles (replace them with their own over time).

At approximately the same time I wrote for the thyroid disease website, a patient support forum in the UK who also had a connecting content article site, asked me to write a few eBooks for them, that they could offer their site members at a cost (to help pay for their own website hosting).

They agreed to pay me a percent on sales if I could provide the eBooks to be advertised on their site. It was also during this time that I created my own website, after gaining some knowledge of editing and HTML from the thyroid disease site editorship I held for nearly two years. This self-published website would also be one that had thyroid disease as its main subject. The site would be for free reading to the public and I would not make it a revenue website at all. There would be no ads accompanying the content-articles and I would pay a hosting fee for it, out of pocket.

The reason I was involving myself in these venues with most of them paying nothing to me, was due to my passion for helping fellow patients to better understand their diseases. I had already seen other fellow patients become terribly discouraged when their treatments didn't provide them enough symptom relief to obtain them a better quality of life and I actually knew of patients who committed suicide due to their disease (i.e. from struggles with severe depression and/or anxiety symptoms).

The fact is that I too had become suicidal at certain points during my own disease symptoms-struggles of mainly chronic fatigue, as my wife is well aware. After more disease manifestations and diagnoses began to arise in my own case, including development of liver disease, nutritional deficiencies and peripheral neuropathy, my medical expenses accumulated to the extent that it required me to cancel the website with a hosting fee and to begin submitting my articles to revenue sharing content websites.

One of the paying websites I wrote for, is known for its strict editorial oversight and articles that are published there, must meet that standard or they are continually sent back to authors until all corrections and changes are made as required for publishing (if they are not initially rejected outright). I worked extremely hard on the articles that were accepted for publishing at this website, numbering 126 content pieces. After the site ran my articles live for 5 years, I asked that they be removed, so that I could compile them into books and eBooks and they granted me this release.

One thing that amazed me, is that once these Editor's Choice winning articles were in book form, I received a few negative reviews on some of the book/eBook titles, they were compiled into. Not only did I receive awards for this content when it was online as articles but dozens of readers posted comments under them, saying they were the best pieces on the subjects they covered, that they had ever read. There are several things I learned from this seeming contradiction, one being that books for purchase, as opposed to free articles, have much harsher critics for them. I also learned that there are less-than-honest reviewers out there (sometimes other authors), who will review books in an overboard negative fashion, for unethical reasons or simply **just because they can** (no consequences for them and they can hide behind user-name identities).

There will likely be additional readers of this book/ebook, who will be offended at what they read on these pages however, if I may help to offset any unnecessary insecurities or feelings of being insulted by reviewers, let me end this chapter with the statements following. ---

19

I know for a fact and have never doubted the fact that there are honest, ethical and high quality reviewers out there and that this type makes up the majority who are members of social media type book reviews websites. This book however, is <u>specifically</u> about **problems** in the field of book reviewing, so please bear this in mind as you continue to each succeeding chapter. Thank you.

2. HIGHLY NEGATIVE BOOK REVIEWS: DESTROYING AUTHORS WITH A FEW TAPS OF THE KEYBOARD

Ongoing concerns have been expressed by indie publishers like me (independents) in regard to "shill"/"troll" reviews for our books and eBooks (highly unfavorable ones) that we see being posted on bookseller websites and I wanted to express some opinions in regard to this issue. Like most other publishers who've been selling their authored titles for relatively long periods of time or who have many titles listed on major bookseller websites (both apply to me), I have received a few of the "hit reviews" myself. I say "hit" as in the sense of making a hit on something in attempt to basically kill it for whatever reasons, not excluding competing authors, trying to gain an advantage for their works by attempting to degrade the written works of other same-genre authors (God help dishonest authors for resorting to this type thing).

There are also 'fans' of other authors who feel they're helping their preferred writers of perfection by posting negative reviews on competitor's books or it can be close friends or family members of other authors who do so. Another scenario I would mention is that it can simply be mean-spirited people, who feel that life or certain circumstances have cheated them in some way and they choose a book-author to vent their frustrations toward. In some cases these types of readers, are looking for a level of perfection and divine or near-divine inspiration in authored works they read and if they fall short and a book or eBook didn't change their lives to the extent expected, they will place a lashing review against it.

In my case, I have written mostly information eBooks and books and those I have published on health and business subjects, among others. These do not usually have story lines and are not offered necessarily as works of inspiration. They offer very good information however, that can provide newbies to particular subjects especially, with a good basic education on them.

The ones I price at $2.99, are usually in the 6,000 to 7,000 word length category. Some have compiled information within them that can of course also be found in 'similarity of content', online but not without a considerable deal of search to find each aspect covered.

If books/eBooks had to all contain a certain high level of extreme inspiration and life-changing content, rather than some of them simply containing very good information that fills a need, the book and eBook seller's shelves would be relatively bare indeed. The fact is that many people buy content books simply because they need to learn about certain aspects of a subject that's new to them. In many cases they prefer a basic rundown and not an elongated, extremely-detailed dissertation with unnecessary filler-details but they do want some length to an information source as well and I feel 6,500 words for example, that covers all major and important aspects of a subject, is absolutely worth $2.99 -- less than a cup of specialty coffee at Starbuck's.

With this said, I can understand when badly-written books receive negative reviews and those lacking content-compared-to-cost. I also understand when bookseller websites want to please customers by letting their reviews stand because as the saying goes: "the customer is always right". What I do feel the screening-staff of reviews for online book outlets should consider however, is that this type stance of allowing <u>all reviews</u>, can be taken to an extreme, simply to keep customers from being angered and discontinuing their shopping, should their review not be approved. Authors after all, are customers too in many cases and a degree of fairness in regard to reviews, should be considered for them as well.

I'll give two examples of reviews placed on eBooks at bookseller websites, to demonstrate the "review allowance" being taken too far in my opinion, respectfully:

In one review I have seen online, a customer uses the heading: "Don't waste your money!", in regard to an eBook they read.

The reviewer goes on to name other author's books of the same genre, adding to it that customers should instead buy those books. This not only is inappropriate but is also categorically "spam" (using a review to advertise other products – a TOS violation for some online sellers).

On another online review I found that was for a book in paperback form, I read where a customer stated that they received the wrong inside file with the correct outside cover when they ordered (the inside was for another paperback). The person commended the bookseller for allowing a return on the incorrect item but they placed a one-star rating on the book and a bad review based on first appearances for the inside content of **the wrong title they received**, saying to the effect: "while I didn't read the book I received by mistake, it didn't look good to me and seemed a bit short on pages". Please understand that I recognize the fact that these type errors regarding POD books (Publish on Demand), are bound to happen occasionally.

I feel it was inappropriate however, for the customer to vent their frustration toward a book they had not actually read and their review should not have been allowed for posting.

These, in my opinion are two examples of reviews that should definitely meet a criterion for those that must be removed or disallowed to begin with (screened out). I sincerely believe that bookseller sites need to tweak their guidelines a bit in regard to reviews like the two I just described that were allowed. It's pretty much a guarantee that many authors have/are experiencing similar scenarios regarding extremely unfair reviews and I honestly believe it would be advantageous to booksellers, as well as to authors, for slightly stricter screening of bogus, spam and attack reviews because that's exactly what some of them are that can apparently make it past some of the current guidelines screenings.

3. A BAD REVIEW ON MY HEALTH TITLE

I received one particular negative review by a customer for an eBook I authored regarding a health disorder and its treatments, in which the reviewer claims that I have a strong message against a certain type of medical treatment. It is literally an incorrect claim they make (although 'possibly' not purposeful but incorrectly perceived on their part) and they state to the effect "WARNING, this eBook contains a strong anti-____ message in it !"(the blank representing a medical treatment they purported that I am against). The amazing thing about this review, is the fact that I'm not only <u>not</u> against the treatment they claim I am against but I actually talk about how much it benefits those who it is administered to, under the correct circumstances, within its pages (backed by reputable medical research sources and studies).

Even my eBook description mentions the treatment and the only precautions I mention, are that it needs to be overseen by a qualified medical doctor.

This is the statement the customer perceived as an "anti-treatment" message and so I'm left with an incorrect statement being applied the eBook review, due to a reader who misunderstood what was stated on the pages in front of them. The person goes on to say to the effect "but if you want a really good book on this subject read so-and-so's book titled "____" (the blank representing their advertisement for another author's book). I'll add that even when books reviewed, show "verified purchase", (as the title of mine I just described showed) this **does not** mean that it was not purchased to be purposefully reviewed negatively for whatever reasons (for a predetermined purpose). Even intentional attack reviewers are willing to make a book purchase, in order to degrade a book/eBook, especially when it is priced at $2.99 or lower. They know that the purchase will add legitimacy to their "hit" against an author. I have attack reviews on some of my titles and the profile of the reviewer shows them to be the only ones to their credit. A customer registering a profile to add only one review in a 2 year period, in itself should send up a red flag to bookseller websites.

4. ARE AUTHOR COMPLAINTS ABOUT NEGATIVE REVIEWS LEGITIMATE?

My concern is that the administrations of book/eBook sellers sites believe we authors who complain about unfair reviews, simply don't want to see negative ones being posted on our live items but this is not completely true, especially not in all cases. If a review is deserved, serious authors will use it as inspiration to improve in the areas of their writing, that are complained about and I believe this to be true in my case.

I am an author of health titles largely and the very same thyroid disease subject eBooks of mine for example, that customers placed 1-star ratings on, previously resulted in a university medical research group, writing to request use of the eBooks, in a class they were teaching (I granted the permission). An eBook I received a 1-star bash review on, that discusses unusual chronic anxiety symptoms (i.e. depersonalization, derealization and catastrophic thoughts), resulted in a PhD doctor writing me to ask how I treated my patients.

I had to let him know that I am a layperson and <u>not</u> a mental health professional or an MD. One of my titles on religion that I received a 1-star bash review on, previously resulted in a lifetime minister (now retired and in his late 70s), telling me that it was my best Christian Bible study and the best he had ever read on the subject.

My authored thyroid information resources also resulted in my being accepted as a writer at two of the largest content websites online and in my being featured by the nation's most well-know thyroid patient advocate -- Mary Shomon, via her write-ups about me on her About.com website. Mrs. Shomon also sent me a half dozen of her New York Times best sellers, for me to review (Dr. Mark Starr MD sent me his book on "hypothyroidism type 2" to review as well). I suppose my bottom line is to say that we who have professional backing, as far as our being assured by reputable reviewers that our written-resources are quality and professional, find it disheartening that John Doe and Jane Doe readers can cast great aspersions against our products, with the simple tapping of their keyboards.

Can these type reviews be merited in some cases? -- **Yes they can** but when they obviously are not merited and a motive such as jealousy or competing titles is possibly involved, what defense do we have? The fact is, that our ability to reciprocate against hit man type reviews is very limited, especially when moderation/screening for them is somewhat lacking.

5. AUTHORS IMPROVE BUT MUST BE OPEN TO 'APPROPRIATE' CRITICISM

Authors must have starting points and if they stick with their craft, their works improve over time as mine have (several unbiased people have let me know this about my work). I'll use the Beatles, my favorite rock group who I discovered as a teen in the 1970s, as an example of improving within a professional craft over time, from an obvious starting point. In about '62 and '63, when the group first launched big as professional musicians, they recorded a few clinker songs here and there (also many great ones) but what a huge transition occurred even within the next couple years as they continued recording new works of rock music. They put out the Sgt. Pepper album in '67 and titles like Abbey Road in '69 (I have a book and eBook title published on the Beatles BTW). Occasionally, they still made a few clinkers in between their many triumphs. Their "Magical Mystery Tour" movie for example, received very bad reviews (although the music album was fantastic).

I point this out because the public in general didn't throw the rock group under a bus because of their occasional shortcomings but some reviewers of books/eBooks, seemingly try to tear an author down literally, over a book they don't like by them ("throwing the baby out with the bathwater" as the saying goes). I can take my hard knocks when they are deserved; if I couldn't I would have started complaining years ago, when I was first attacked for something I had written online or within books/eBooks. I will add that reviews should be directed at a reader's experience with the content of a book and not at authors personally. Some booksellers actually state this as a TOS guideline for reviews and derogatory statements toward authors are not permitted.

When I see reader-complaints regarding grammar, spelling, formatting or typos of various types, I immediately go to the book file in question and I improve these areas in every way possible. I see these types of complaints as constructive, although I have at times searched for errors listed by a reader but not be able to find them.

I would also have 2 to 3 other people who are prolific readers and/or fellow-writers, to search through the files as well and they-too were unable to identify the reported errors. In these cases, the reader was either mistaken about the typos or they were reporting them for bogus reasons. Additionally, the major bookseller I first publish new titles through, has a program in place that is very thorough in checking for typos. I will not publish a new title, until any typos discovered by the program are corrected. It is for these reasons, that typos and misspellings reported by readers are researched by me and I believe this to be the case with most authors who are wanting to improve their writing skills.

6. VAGUE REVIEWS NOT EXPLAINING WHY A LOW RATING WAS GIVEN

I have my own commentary and interpretations on Christian Bible study subjects that I have published since the late 1990s, which are based on some of the more controversial biblical teachings but that cover very intriguing aspects of them. I specifically state in the description of some of these, that they were written in simplistic terms so that a non-theologian can understand them and yet I still had a reader come along in a review and state to the effect regarding a couple of my shorter length works (about 7,000 words each): "this book lacked the scholarly level I was looking for". It literally made me wonder why this man bought these eBooks with my description not only stating them to be written on a layman's level but I also state within the description, that those seeking a more comprehensive study, should take advantage of my title on the same subject that is four times the length and goes into much greater detail, which I referred to specifically within the description, by title-name.

I make both types of books/eBooks available (the shorter, less comprehensive and the more-detailed, lengthy comprehensive ones) not only on biblical subjects but also for titles I have on health and business. I learned back in about the year 2004, that there are people who want **both types** of information-providing resources and in fact my shorter ones outsell my lengthier ones by at least 5 to 1. I also wondered if it was possible that the man who posted the complaining-review, was an author with his own titles available. Unusual things in reviews like these, makes one think they should be more specific if the reader feels there is actually a problem. Instructions to reviewers such as those stating: "If you feel a book lacked content on the subject it was written on, please specifically describe what you feel was missing within the subject matter." These type suggestions would likely turn off the trolls to some degree (illegitimate reviewers), from posting their attack reviews because they would then realize that posting one simply to vent because they had a bad day or for some other bogus reason, would be transparent and lacking true purpose.

How a reviewer thinks I could improve an eBook by saying "it didn't have in it what I wanted", always make me sit back in my computer chair asking myself "What is that statement supposed to mean?" and "What was this person's real motive behind the unfavorable review? ...Was the motivation from unreal expectations, legitimate complaints, a competing author or someone who simply enjoys knocking down the efforts of others?"

I absolutely am not against getting an unfavorable review when it is merited but what further confirms one to be bogus is when you have a title highly-praised by other readers (unsolicited positive reviews), plus you have the intelligence to know for a fact that a title hits the mark in providing quality information/reading. More specifics on negative reviews is a logical thing for authors to desire from unsatisfied readers.

7. TRASH TITLES CONTRIBUTE TO BAD PERCEPTIONS TOWARD INDIE AUTHORS

In regard to trash titles being submitted to booksellers and sometimes being published by them, I believe this can no doubt negatively affect the perception of indie authors overall but initial screening by publishing platforms should catch these inferior written works and screen them out (this is not always the case). I mentioned previously about having dozens of titles of my own published and I'll repeat the fact that most of mine are health-related. I have written a great deal about diseases that have affected my own life (i.e. thyroid disease, peripheral neuropathy, chronic fatigue syndrome, etc...). And yes, in spite of the occasional complaint that non medical professionals are writing books on medical/health subjects, there are readers who want to read information from fellow patients, who are experiencing their same diseases first-hand ("patient advocates").

My other major venue is Christian Bible subjects as also previously mentioned, with the third being business titles (none were public domain but all self-authored by me). When I publish a work in book or eBook form, my titles will be a minimum of 6,000 words average but some are 12,000, 30,000, 40,000 or even over 150,000 words in length. I do however keep mine in that lower range, so that I can #1. Retail them at a lower price, affordable to more readers and #2. So that I can price them at a retail that meets a royalty-earning category required by certain sellers but that is still the lowest possible retail for the amount of content. Unfortunately (and what I'm about to say, I've heard many other publishers report), some readers actually believe a 6,500 word eBook for example, is priced too-high at "$2.99" and they will give a bad review for one, by including the shortness of the content as a reason for it. I would disagree with this view regarding shorter subject eBooks and to offer some perspective, I would add that I bought a coffee latte at Starbuck's recently that took me approximately 10 minutes to drink, at a cost of $3.50 plus tax!

One of my $2.99 eBooks, might take only an hour to read but it will contain top-notch information -- although I admit I often don't cover more than the most important information in many of them (nothing important excluded but with no unnecessary fillers added). If I could retail my eBook titles at for a lower price, such as "$1.99" and earn the amount of royalty I need, I would do so and I would have mine priced with all retailers at the same lowered price. I can't do this however because I cut my royalty percent in half at my largest selling outlets, who have a certain royalty structure in place. I do believe a lower threshold for higher royalty percentages, would let me retail my titles at a better customer response and satisfaction but I cannot be overly-biased toward my own wants or needs and I have to consider the needs of the book/eBook platforms who allow me to publish and sell through them. At the same time I also don't want to compromise the value of my work, so here again, I have a dilemma without a perfect solution but I do the best I can, considering that booksellers have to make a profit that makes their publishing platforms worthwhile to them. This keeps us both going.

8. IN CONCLUSION:

In light of the preceding information I have offered, I would suggest that bookseller websites can find ways to prevent negative reviews that are imbalanced in the ways they are written, from occurring or from being accepted for display on the products they represent in their online stores. Each bookseller will of course have their own uniquely-designed set of guidelines in place however, some suggestions I would make, include not allowing reviews to be posted for a certain period of time after a new book or eBook product is listed. This would not need to be for an extended period of time but possibly one that is 3 to 6 months in duration, so that purchases versus returns on a product, can be gauged to see if they correlate with the types of reviews that are posted afterward, once allowed. A product that sells 100 units but that only has 2 returns within the same period of time, would indicate that there is a general public acceptance for it. A bookseller would then know that it is a product they should continue to carry and one they should open for reviews.

Please understand, this is purely an off-the-cuff example and I am simply trying to show that more structuring of some type could be in place regarding the TOS/TOU for reviews.

I would also suggest that online booksellers ask reviewers not to use excessive negative language and that they should use examples of improper statements within their guidelines, such as reviews stating things such as "Don't waste your time" or "Spend your money elsewhere", will not be allowed. Readers can vary greatly in their evaluation of a book -- a common sense reason to disallow overboard comments.

Personal attacks toward an author should be disallowed as well, such as making references to their lack of education or questioning their calling to become an author. Such guidelines could include statements to the effect that the bookseller has done a pre-screening of book and eBooks and that they have met their own guidelines for acceptance within their product lines.

A bookseller can always make the point clear, that they are not asking that unfavorable reviews not be posted but that they are stated reasonably respectfully, rather than in an attacking, degrading, insulting or harassing manner. This is already stated similarly in some bookseller's TOS guidelines for reviewers. This will prevent a growing trend from occurring in which there is an "anything goes" mentality in regard to book reviewing (under the guise of "free speech" and "freedom of expression" – a privilege that still has legal boundaries). It will also prevent discouragement from occurring within the minds of aspiring authors who are sincere about their craft and who simply seek the opportunity to improve their skills and to grow their base of written works for the enjoyment and benefit of interested readers.

Some history behind the purpose of this book/ebook:

I have stayed up-to-date on concerns being expressed by fellow authors, on the associated publisher's forums of booksellers.

From the very beginning of my checking in to read at these (but with very infrequent posting of my own), I saw where publishers were complaining frequently about reviews that were designed not to express displeasure and dissatisfaction with books of theirs that customers had read but reviews with obvious intent to degrade a written work for other reasons. This included simply spam reviews, ones that obviously were posted with purposeful obscenity and those that didn't stop at stating dissatisfaction with books but that went on to attack, degrade and to indirectly harass and defame the authors of them. The complaints by authors about these type reviews have continued to be frequent from the beginning of my checking in at bookseller publisher's forums. With this being the case, I wanted to address the subject in a short subject book of my own.

THE REASON THIS SUBJECT WAS NECESSARILY ADDRESSED:

I have received these type reviews myself but infrequently.

I made my first complaint on a review in late 2012 (it was not one for this title and was my first complaint in nearly 5 years). Some of these were removed by the bookseller websites (A fact showing that inappropriate reviews do occur). I have in-fact had reviews removed by two major booksellers but I did not request these particular removals (they detected unethical elements in them). Reviewers who have already posted their reviews on this book title have expressed the opinion that there is NO PROOF that unfair reviews take place or that they may be the first posted, long before positive reviews appear for published books but this scenario does take place. A reviewer for a controversial book on the subject of creationism titled: "In the Beginning: Compelling Evidence for Creation and the Flood" (By: Walter T. Brown) states this in their review of the book: QUOTE: "From this category of books I usually select those which have a lot of 1 star reviews. I wasn't wrong this time either. The enemies of truth, for whatever reasons, are very active and jump in immediately with bad comments, against a good strong book" :END OF QUOTE

I want it to be very clear that I believe in most cases, 1-star dissatisfied writers of reviews are being completely honest in their negative evaluations for books but there can be other motives as well, including reviews posted by dishonest, competing authors or simply by mean-spirited people who enjoy attempting to degrade the efforts of others. These are the type that I have seen removed by booksellers sites, at their own discretion. The dishonest motives for reviews are usually apparent (not always) by the fact that these type usually contain a great deal of sarcasm, insults, harassing remarks and attempts at defamation toward authors. How can these types of elements be considered even remotely a part of honest reviewing and especially that of purported professional reviewing?

In the case of this short-subject book I wrote in regard to "undeserved", "unfair" reviews, I was warned by fellow-publishers that some reviewers would take offense to the subject being addressed.

They would feel their rights to review in any way they choose would be threatened (especially those who are members of social-media reviewing websites). THEY WERE RIGHT, however, this was not my intention. My intention was rather to help bring balance and perspective to the subject in my own limited way and to offer a few suggestions in regard to the moderating of reviews at bookseller websites, as I attempted to do so.

-*Jim Lowrance*

www.ingramcontent.com/pod-product-compliance
Lightning Source LLC
Chambersburg PA
CBHW061520180526
45171CB00001B/263